2006 RSJA Grant
Wed + Fred

3/8/06 Raintree #28.21

Earthquakes and Volcanoes

and

Volcanoes

A Survival Guide

Chicago, Illinois

Raintree

Customer Service   888–363–4266

Visit our website at www.heinemannraintree.com

Printed and bound in the United States by Lake Book
Manufacturing, Inc.

10 09 08 07 06
10 9 8 7 6 5 4 3 2 1

**Library of Congress Cataloging-in-
Publication Data**
Townsend, John, 1955-
  Earthquakes and volcanoes – a survival guide:
Earth's physical processes / John Townsend.
     p. cm. -- (Fusion)
  Includes bibliographical references and index.
  ISBN 1-4109-1927-7 (library binding-hardcover) --
ISBN 1-4109-1958-7
(pbk.)
 1. Earthquakes--Juvenile literature. 2. Volcanoes--
Juvenile
literature.
 I. Title. II. Fusion (Chicago, Ill.)
  QE521.3.T69 2005
  363.34'95--dc22
                                         2005011088

Acknowledgments
The author and publishers are grateful to the
following for permission to reproduce copyright
material: Alamy Images/AM Corporation pp. 22–23;
Alamy Images pp. 26–27 (Adrian Arbib); Corbis p. 13;
Corbis/Reuters p. 15 (bottom); Corbis/Reuters p. 11
(bottom) (Yuriko Nakao); The Kobal Collection/
Universal pp. 4–5; Science Photo Library p. 11 (top);
Science Photo Library pp. 16–17 (Jeremy Bishop), 15
(top) (Gary Hincks), 6–7 (Ken M. Johns), 21 (right)
(Peter Menzel), 29 (David Parker), 24–25 (Dr Morley
Read), 18–19 (David Weintraub), 21 (left) (Ed Young).

Cover photograph of Los Angeles cityscape,
reproduced with permission of Getty Images/Taxi.

Illustrations by Darren Lingard.

The publishers would like to thank Nancy Harris
and Harold Pratt for their assistance in the
preparation of this book.

Every effort has been made to contact copyright
holders of any material reproduced in this book.
Any omissions will be rectified in subsequent
printings if notice is given to the publishers.

The paper used to print this book comes from
sustainable resources.

Contents

Some words are printed in bold, **like this**. You can find out what they mean on page 30. You can also look in the box at the bottom of the page where they first appear.

What on Earth Is Happening?

"It was only a murmur at first. The sound seemed far away. What was going on? Soon, it sounded like a train passing through the house. The floor started to move and rumble. Everything began to shake. The room swayed.

"The TV fizzed and went out with a pop. By now, the noise was a thundering roar. Books fell off the shelves. Then, the shelves themselves fell down. There were thuds all through the house. This was scary! This was an earthquake!"

This person was describing how it feels to be caught in an earthquake. Would you know what to do in an earthquake? One day you may need to know.

▼The scene in this photo is from a movie about an earthquake.

5

The power of earthquakes

When a big earthquake strikes, the ground shakes. It shakes so much that buildings fall down. Cracks appear in the roads. Bridges can break.

Earthquakes are not always dangerous, though. Sometimes Earth only moves a little. This is called a **tremor**.

Volcanoes often **erupt** where earthquakes happen. Volcanoes are cone-shaped mountains or hills. A volcano can throw up liquid rock, or **lava**, from deep inside Earth.

To be safe from earthquakes and volcanoes, you need answers to some questions:

- Why do earthquakes and volcanoes happen?
- Where are the most dangerous places?
- What are the warning signs?
- What should you do if a volcano erupts near you?

Read on to find the answers!

erupt	to break through a surface and burst out
lava	melted rock that comes out of a volcano
tremor	small earthquake

▼ This huge crack in Earth's surface was caused by an earthquake in California.

Did you know?

- In 1556 an earthquake killed over 800,000 people in China.

- In 1815 a volcano killed 90,000 people in Indonesia.

Inside Earth

What causes earthquakes to happen and volcanoes to **erupt**? To understand, we have to look at the way Earth is made.

Earth is a bit like an egg. It has:

- A **crust** (a thin outer shell)
- A **mantle** (a thick layer of hot rock below the crust. In some places, the rock melts. The liquid rock is called **magma**.)
- A **core** (the center of Earth).

Earth's crust is cracked into large pieces. If an egg shell is cracked, the insides ooze out through the cracks. In the same way, liquid magma can ooze out through Earth's crust. This happens in places where the crust is very cracked or thin. These are the places where volcanoes form.

This picture shows the ▶ inside of Earth.

core	central part of Earth
crust	outer part of Earth
magma	hot liquid rock in Earth's mantle and crust
mantle	thick layer of rock between Earth's crust and the core

The large pieces of Earth's crust can move around. These movements are what cause earthquakes. Earthquakes and volcanoes tend to happen near the cracks in Earth's crust.

crust

core

mantle

Restless Earth

The huge pieces that make up Earth's **crust** are called **plates**. These plates rest or "float" on top of the **mantle**.

The mantle is like thick, liquid plastic. It moves very slowly. The slowly moving mantle makes the plates move, too.

Plates may:

- Move apart from each other
- Push into each other
- Slide slowly past each other.

The edges of the plates are jagged. The edges may stick together for a long time. Then, creak . . . crunch . . . BANG! They suddenly scrape past each other. This is when an earthquake happens.

If an earthquake happens under the sea, it can cause huge waves, called **tsunamis**. Tsunamis can travel for hundreds of miles over the ocean.

plate   huge moving piece of Earth's crust
tsunami   great sea wave made by an earthquake under the sea

Earth's plates

Eurasian Plate

North American Plate

Eurasian Plate

Arabian Plate

Pacific Plate

Cocos Plate

Nazca Plate

South American Plate

African Plate

Indo-Australian Plate

Antarctic Plate

▲ *The orange lines on this world map show the edges of some of Earth's plates.*

Did you know?

At the end of 2004, an underwater earthquake caused a huge tsunami. Giant waves swept across the Indian Ocean. Over 200,000 people died.

11

Danger Zone: Ring of Fire

The biggest of Earth's **plates** is the Pacific Ocean plate. It is as big as the Pacific Ocean.

Most of Earth's earthquakes and volcanoes happen around the edges of the Pacific plate. Earthquakes happen where two plates are moving past each other.

Volcanoes burst through cracks in Earth's **crust**. There are so many volcanoes around the edges of the Pacific plate that it is called the Ring of Fire.

Ring of Fire

China
Japan
The Philippines
Indonesia
North America
Ring of Fire
South America
Australia
Indian Ocean
Pacific Ocean

The red dots on the map on page 12 show where volcanoes are along the Ring of Fire. It is not easy for people living in these places to avoid earthquakes and volcanoes.

▼ Smoke often pours out of volcanoes along the Ring of Fire.

Warning Signs

Scientists cannot always tell when earthquakes will strike. Yet sometimes they can warn that an earthquake will happen soon. Scientists use an instrument called a **seismograph** to measure earthquakes.

In 1975 scientists in China were sure an earthquake was going to happen. No one could feel the **tremors**. Instead, a seismograph sensed them. Scientists gave a warning. The next day, an earthquake hit Haicheng in China. Because of the warning, people left the city. Many lives were saved.

A year later, another earthquake struck without warning near Haicheng. It killed about 250,000 people.

Did you know?

San Francisco, California, was almost destroyed by an earthquake in 1906. In 1989 another earthquake struck the same area. Scientists think that another big earthquake will hit the city in the next 30 years.

seismograph instrument used to measure and record movements of Earth

Case

Pen

Roll of paper

▼ *A seismograph is fixed to the ground. In an earthquake, the case and the roll of paper move around. The pen stays still. It draws the pattern of the earthquake on the roll of paper.*

Volcano alert!

Scientists can often tell when a volcano is about to **erupt**. A volcano is fixed in one place so it is easier to study. Photographs taken from space can show volcanoes changing shape. This happens before they erupt.

Scientists who study volcanoes are called **volcanologists**. They climb onto volcanoes. They measure changes in the ground.

A volcano throws out liquid rock called **lava**. Lava is boiling hot! Volcanologists need to wear heat suits to be safe.

A heat suit will not protect scientists against lava bombs. These are huge lumps of melted rock that shoot into the air. Hot ash and deadly gases can suddenly shoot out, too.

volcanologist   scientist who studies volcanoes

▼ *Studying an active volcano can be a very dangerous job!*

Without warning

Sometimes volcanoes **erupt** without warning. On Sunday, May 18, 1980, Mount St. Helens erupted. This volcano is in Washington State.

Ten minutes earlier, an earthquake had shaken the volcano. It made the north face of the mountain fall away. This caused the biggest **landslide** ever known. Tons of earth and ice crashed down into Spirit Lake nearby.

Gases had built up inside the volcano. Then, the north slope of the volcano fell away. The **pressure** inside the volcano was released. It was like a cork popping out of a bottle.

Survivor's story

On May 18, 1980, Jim Scymanky and three other men were cutting wood in a forest near Mount St. Helens. Jim described how "a horrible, crunching, grinding sound" came through the trees. Suddenly, the air was full of hot, black ash. They were all badly burned. Jim was the only survivor.

landslide   when a mass of rocks or earth slips down a steep slope
pressure   force pushing against a surface

▼ When Mount St. Helens erupted, 57 people were killed.

Measuring the Power

Many earthquakes and volcanoes rumble all the time. They are not all dangerous.

Earthquakes come in different strengths. They can be small **tremors** or great mega-quakes. Scientists measure how strong an earthquake is on a scale. It is called the **Richter Scale**. It gives an earthquake a score between 1 and 9.

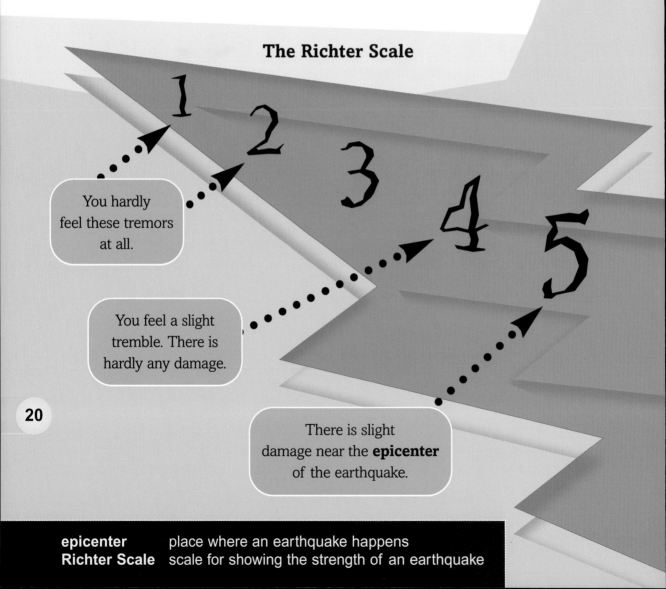

The Richter Scale

You hardly feel these tremors at all.

You feel a slight tremble. There is hardly any damage.

There is slight damage near the **epicenter** of the earthquake.

epicenter   place where an earthquake happens
Richter Scale   scale for showing the strength of an earthquake

California
1994

Mexico City
1985

There is serious damage 62 miles (100 kilometers) from the epicenter.

There is huge damage. Many people are killed over hundreds of miles.

Mega-quakes like this do not happen often. There is massive damage over thousands of miles.

6

7

8

9

There is damage to buildings within 6.2 miles (10 kilometers) of the epicenter.

Safe Building

If you live in an earthquake zone, you need a well-built house. No building can be completely safe from earthquakes. However, all buildings can be made safer. They need to be built with extra-strong materials.

In earthquake zones, many buildings are built on special pads. These pads can move with the shaking Earth. This stops the buildings from falling down. Some homes in Japan and the United States are built this way.

A special bridge

The Akashi-Kaikyo bridge in Japan was specially built to cope with earthquakes. The bridge should stay standing in earthquakes that measure up to 8.5 on the **Richter Scale**!

After-Effects

The earthquake is over. The shaking has stopped. Is everything safe now? No, it is not!

Everywhere there are broken electricity wires and broken gas pipes. These can cause injury, death, or serious fires. There are broken water pipes, too. Dirty water soon spreads disease. This is a very dangerous time.

Did you know that volcanoes can even change the weather? In 1815 the volcano Tambora **erupted** in Indonesia. The next year was known as the "year without a summer." Tambora threw out thick clouds of ash. The sunlight could not get through these clouds.

The biggest bang

*One of the biggest volcanic eruptions was Krakatoa in Indonesia. In 1883 it blew apart a whole island. It caused a **tsunami** that killed 36,000 people. A thick cloud of ash rose 50 miles (80 kilometers) into the sky. It affected the world's weather for several years.*

This is Quito, the capital of Ecuador. In 2002 the volcano Reventador erupted nearby. It filled the air with ash. People needed face masks to help them breathe.

25

Survival

Learning about earthquakes and volcanic eruptions can help to keep you safe. It is important to know what to do if they happen. However, you do not always have to worry about them.

Remember that most earthquakes are so small you cannot feel them. Many others do nothing more than rattle the windows.

Did you know that volcanoes can sometimes be good for you?

Some people live close to volcanoes. They do this because ash from volcanoes makes good, rich soil. The rich soil is good for growing crops. Also, streams on volcanoes can be hot. They give free hot water!

▼ People can live very well near volcanoes. The soil around a volcano is rich and good for farming.

Be Prepared

In an earthquake, you are in danger of getting hurt by falling buildings. Follow this advice to keep as safe as possible:

DROP down to the floor.

Take **COVER** under a strong piece of furniture.

HOLD onto the furniture. Be ready to move with it until the ground stops shaking and it is safe to come out.

REMEMBER

- If you are in a HIGH BUILDING, and you are not near a table, go to an inside wall. Protect your head with your arms.

- If you are OUTDOORS, move away from trees, buildings, or wires.

- If you are NEAR BUILDINGS, duck into a doorway. Protect yourself from falling bricks.

- Be prepared for further earthquakes called AFTERSHOCKS. Take cover when they happen.

(Based on advice from the American Red Cross)

Glossary

core central part of Earth. It is made mostly of the two metals, iron and nickel.

crust outer part of Earth. The crust is made of solid rock. It is between 6.2 and 31 miles (10 and 50 kilometers) thick.

epicenter place where an earthquake happens. The epicenter is the point on Earth's surface that is directly above where an earthquake starts.

erupt to break through a surface and burst out. Volcanoes erupt every year around the world.

landslide when a mass of rocks or earth slides down a steep slope. Landslides can be caused by earthquakes. They can also be caused by very heavy rain.

lava melted rock that comes out of a volcano. When lava cools, it hardens into solid rock.

magma hot liquid rock in Earth's mantle. Magma rises up through Earth's crust and comes through the mouth of a volcano as lava.

mantle thick layer of rock between Earth's crust and the core. In some places, the mantle is so hot that it is melted. This is where volcanoes happen.

plate huge moving piece of Earth's crust. Earthquakes and volcanoes often happen where plates meet.

pressure force pushing against a surface. Pressure builds up under Earth's crust. This causes earthquakes and volcanoes.

Richter Scale scale for showing the strength of an earthquake. It measures the strength with scores from 1 to 9. The strongest is 9.

seismograph instrument used to measure and record movements of Earth. This can tell scientists how powerful an earthquake is.

tremor small earthquake. Tremors often happen before or after a big earthquake.

tsunami great sea wave made by an earthquake under the sea. Tsunamis are rare, but they can cause terrible damage when they strike a coast.

volcanologist scientist who studies volcanoes

Want to Know More?

Books to read

- Colson, Mary. *Crumbling Earth: Erosion and Landslides.* Chicago: Raintree, 2006.

- Lassieur, Allison. *Volcanoes.* Mankato, Minn.: Capstone, 2001.

- Spilsbury, Louise and Richard. *Shattering Earthquakes.* Chicago: Heinemann Library, 2004.

Websites

- http://www.fema.gov/kids/dizarea.htm

  Do you want to learn more about earthquakes and volcanoes? Check out this exciting website to play games and take quizzes! Sponsored by the Federal Emergency Management Agency.

Find out more about restless Earth and how it can affect our weather in *Disappearing Mountain and Other Earth Mysteries.*

Rocks can be a lot more exciting than you might think! Find out why in *Tales of a Prehistoric Sponge.*

Index